# Magic The Gathering

Deck Building For Beginners (MTG, Deck Building, Strategy)

Alexander Norland

If you find this book helpful, please leave a review on Amazon here. It will help others also find this book.

# Table of Contents

# 1 - Introduction

## Getting Started

This book can be seen as a basic guide to building a deck for "Magic The Gathering". The goal of this book is to teach you the basic, guiding principles that will assist you in having the strongest deck possible when going into a battle against another player. The following chapters will take a piece of the process and allow an in-depth description of how and why you should make choices to build the strongest deck.

After reading this book, one should be able to fully understand the basics of "Magic The Gathering" and why different features are important for building different decks.

The aim of this book is to give the reader a comprehensive idea of knowing the format of the game you are playing, determine how you want to play and the color combination you want to use, testing a deck for balance, finding the actual cards or being able to use a card list or card search engine to build your deck list and finally the playtest and how to maximize your sideboard cards.

By the time you have reached the conclusion of this book, I am confident that any reader will have a thorough understanding of how to create a great beginner deck for slaughtering any opponent.

# 2 - Deck Basics

## Choosing A Format

When it comes to the basic rules that help you decide your format, there are a few mainstays that should always be taken into account. A couple of basic rules for formats is that you know your minimum deck size and only having 4 copies of each card that is not a basic land card.

Another basic rule of formatting is that if a card is on the restricted list, a player should only have one copy of that card. If the card is on the banned list, you cannot use that card in a given game.

When it comes to picking a format, there are many different options to choose from. These include formats such as Commander, Legacy and Vintage; however, in beginning to learn the rules of the game and formatting, this book will emphasize:

- Standard

- Modern

- Limited

# Standard Deck

The Standard deck is considered to be the basic deck and is called a Constructed format—essentially meaning that each deck is Constructed, or made up, before the game starts.

It consists of a minimum deck size of 60 cards and only consists of cards from the previous and current blocks as well as the current core set(s) that will be played in the game. Modern deck formation is basically the same as Standard, except for the fact you can use all sets from the 8th edition and after.

# Limited

When it comes to Limited format, the deck is not Constructed before the game begins, players are Drafting. Essentially the drafting format is, as the title would insinuate, drawing or drafting different cards into your deck throughout the game. In this format, players choose 3 15-card booster packs[1] that are passed from player to player throughout the game.

---

[1]http://www.powerlists.org/ny7j

# Deck Size

The minimum deck size in this format is 40, as opposed to 60 in the other two, and players are not restricted to their sideboard or even the 4 copies of limited cards rule.

# 3 - Determining How You Want to Play

## Manner of Attack

After you have decided what Format you would like to use to play, players need to decide on their preferred manner of attack. This will come out in how you wish to play the game against your opponents and determine the colors and types of cards you will use to some extent (we will cover colors in-depth in the next chapter).

## Style Options

The style options for playing are three different archetypes:

- Aggro

- Control

- Combo

This style determines the type of opponent you will be and the control you have over the deck, to some extent, by the types of attacks you will be playing.

# Aggro

First off there is the Aggro style of play that, as the title suggests, is based on the players ability to aggressively attack his or her opponent. The overall aim of this deck is basically to slaughter your opponents with attacks and, in turn, reinforce your strength and build your numbers.

Aggro is generally the simplest type to play; however, with this deck you also get the least number of cards with the ability to protect yourself. This dominantly red color deck can allow a player to have great strength but, when attacked by an opponent, may be left very defenseless.

To strengthen one's deck, there is an option of taking advantage of +1/+1 counters that increase the creatures ability to be tough and powerful. Lastly, an Aggro player can use the token cards that allow for different spells to summon 2 or more creature tokens—allowing for the spells to multiply creatures.

## Control Strategy

Instead of this Aggro philosophy, others may want to place more of a hold over the other players by using the Control strategy. One very key component of this player style is that some cards allow for the player to control and ban different cards played by their opponent.

In addition to this advantage, some control decks have cards with a plethora of counterspells on them—one example is what is referred to as Permission decks. Another aspect of this style is that one can control their opponent's decks by having them play out the important phrase in Magic where one has to "draw a card".

The last of the advantages of control is boardwipe, meaning, one has the power to destroy their opponents creatures or other permanents.

## Mid-Range

One style that is not part of the three main categories is a mix of Aggro and Control styles called Mid-range. This allows for a player to have characteristics of either Aggro or Control either one with just a bit more power than the other.

For example, one could have a largely Control deck but use Aggro features to support the creatures. This allows for one to have spells and controls that feature both archetypes.

# Aggro and Control

The final style takes a combination of Aggro and Control and allows for a player to draw from both in the formation of their deck. In this type of deck, the player can use a powerful creature card and add "cantrips" and "scry" to it to increase and maximize the creatures' power. "Cantrips" are cards that allow for the player to draw more cards and "scry" is using one's top card by keeping it to continuously use.

One could also employ a "Maze End[2]" deck that, if a player has all 10 gates, you automatically win. With all good decks, keep in mind that you should aim for more than 1 winning condition—allowing for artifact cards such as the Door to Nothingness[3].

All three of these archetypes are distinctive in their own way and allow for a player to have a different playing experience in each game. There are also a variety of ways to style your deck with your own personal flavor. As you learn and become more familiar with the cards and their powers, you can personalize a strategy you feel is the most powerful on

---

[2]http://www.powerlists.org/ehrc

[3]http://www.powerlists.org/65om

# 3 - DETERMINING HOW YOU WANT TO PLAY

your opponents.

# 4 - Determining Which Color You Will Use

Choosing a format and then a style of play are the first two steps in "Magic The Gathering" that lead to a player choosing their color combinations in their deck. Coming into talking about the colors of "Magic The Gathering" is a powerful way to explore how important the colors are in representing different types of magic used in the game.

The colors of magic are:

- White

- Blue

- Black

- Red

- Green

These 5 colors make up the different types of enchantments and magic that are played out in the game, through the use of different color combinations.

## White

White, for example, is the color that most represents power and life within the game. This card emphasizes on increasing one's life, increasing one's power, it is a card of help as well as a card that allows one to tap other creatures and yet remain untapped.

## Blue

Blue is the logic and intelligence of the color spectrum. These blue cards are usually played best during an opponent's turn where one can react against an attack. Another advantage of this color is that there are unblockable creatures to play against your opponent. The counterspells on this card react favorably against aggressive decks as well.

## Black

Black is a card that a player will be drawn to if they seek a color that curses opponents, deals got lots of damage and is a fighting card. The ability of deathtouch is one of this group that allows for one to destroy their enemy or the ability of infect allows for damage to an opponent with a -1/-1 poison counter.

# Red

Red is the color that is most representative of an aggressive, Agro style of play. This color tends towards cards that enhance one's attacking of opponents. These types of spells from this color are quintessential to an Aggro style player's deck.

# Green

The last of the colors, green, is a strength based power that allows for an aggressive approach to building strength and growth. Also, as most things of green color would suggest, this color represents a building and strengthening of life.

The enchantments found in this color are instrumental in toughness and power. Features of these enchantments are such things as not allowing an opponent to target you as easily—or that you still can damage the player if they damage you.

From these five colors, one needs to develop a color scheme that best fits with their player's format and style. All of these 3 elements need to be present in order to create the best offense and defense of a player as possible. Most decks people use have 2 colors. However, sometimes starting out it can be useful to use a mono-colored deck to really get to know the advantages of a given color.

# 5 - Testing Your Deck

## Mana Curve

A good feature of the deck you choose is to be able to check the deck's mana curve as well as explore the play you find most attractive to you, in order to properly test the deck. One can think of mana in the game similar to health in a traditional video game—however, this health is how much magical strength (mana) you need in order to be able to impart a spell or creature on your enemy.

This is where the type of deck and colors you choose in your deck come into account. For the purposes of building a basic desk, one has basic lands cards of Plains, Island, Swamp, Mountain and Forest to work with. Each of these cards needs a different mana source to be able to power its functions.

## Attack Style

This is where it's important to understand your attack style and colored cards you fill your deck with. Being able to give yourself the maximum access to mana possible, you increase the chances of your cards working in your favor. Learning how enchantments and mana work is an important part of the game that comes with the more practice in gameplay that you get.

Through the process of beginning to test your deck against other players, the ability to understand how mana works and the amount of mana you need shows you your mana curve. In the last paragraph, the idea of mana balance in a deck was explained. The mana curve is where your deck finds its strength and weaknesses when you build it.

Researching how and why mana in used and needed in the cards is an important building block of playing "Magic The Gathering". Online there is a litany of research material for why and how mana will work for individual decks in theory. You can even look at a category of cards and find websites that walk you through the pros and cons of the cards.

These types of search tools can be found by simply typing a phrase like "magic the gathering card search" into Google (no quotations necessary) and finding a compatible website for you.

## Strength and Types

While you build and find a better understanding of the mana in spells, it's also important to develop a sense of the strength and types of cards that appear on each different color. These types of features found on the cards are things from bombs, removals, evasion, attack, defense and aggro and finally, dud cards.

## Bombs

Bomb cards are those that allow for the player to do damage to their opponent. Typically these bomb cards are seen as creatures in Limited; however, these cards can be helpful in many battle situations. These cards sometimes stand as win conditions in games—an extremely desirable outcome.

## Removals

Removals, unlike bombs adding to a scenario, are cards that typically take away a harmful spell or condition. These cards can start from small removals of negative effects to cards that literally can be called "board wipers" that take an eraser and destroy everything in its path. Just as having a weapon can be the game changer, this can be to take away from the power of those offensive weapons.

## Evasion

Evasion offers players options, when their opponent has

played a card that would typically allow them safety, to break barriers and create damage. These cards would allow for a player to trample through an opponents blocked barrier and cause damage when they thought they were safe against attack.

## Maximizing Attacks

The attack, defensive and aggro allows the player to come up with a game plan they will use against their opponents. The manner of which cards are played, in order to maximize attacks, becomes important in your strategy with these cards. The area of expertise on how and why to use these cards comes with practice or even research into some of the online databases for card search.

## Duds

Unfortunately, there are sometimes cards in a deck that become duds. These cards are not helpful to one's deck as they do not bring any defensive or offensive spell or creature power. For example, having a "Time to Feed[4] " card in your deck that consists of no creatures is not an advantage to the player.

---

[4]http://www.powerlists.org/qyqr

# 6 - How to Obtain and Build Your Deck

When it comes to acquiring cards for "Magic The Gathering" there are opportunities to get cards both online and in retail stores. These days stores like Target and Walgreens even WalMart offer card gamers the opportunity to purchase cards at many locations.

## Comic Book Shops

There are also usually local comic book or gaming shops that offer the player a more informative retail clerk to help them make their gaming card decisions.

## Retail Outlets

Along with the market for cards in retail outlets, one can also turn to many online distributors to purchase cards. In these online retail outlets, there tends to be a larger cornucopia of options for any gamer. These sites can also offer tips on how to play or buy their cards effectively. There is a large portion of gamers themselves who sell decks on eBay and other such stores.

# Google

You can also Google search terms like "Finding Magic the Gathering cards near me" or other similar phrases, or go to the "Magic The Gathering" official website to get a firm idea on where in your area you should look.

# 7 - Your Decks Playtest and Side-board Cards

Now that you have been successfully overwhelmed with how and why to pick a deck, we will now discuss a little about a decks Playtest and Sideboard cards. The most important part of this step is to have a person or persons to play against and test your deck's power against your opponents!

This is a great way to figure out what works for your deck, through how well you do against others and matching up against their decks.

## Sideboard

The sideboard is a very important feature of the game, as it essentially gives you 15 cards to switch out your main deck's cards with. Essentially, this is a card pile you can draw cards from and switch out with those in your main deck.

The catch is that you must draw the same number of cards from both decks when you switch them out. The sideboard feature is for games that are Constructed and have a set amount of cards, as we already have a similar feature built into the Limited format.

With the information gained with each deck you bring to the gauntlet and play with opponents, the more you are able to evolve your playing strategy. The more effort and intellect one puts into developing a deck and sizing up to opponents, the greater and more valuable a deck can become in the world of "Magic The Gathering".

# 8 - Conclusion

## Premium Deck Building

The goal of this book was to teach the reader a comprehensive approach to choosing a premium "Magic The Gathering" deck. This book has hopefully served as a beginner's guide that will help you through the game as you develop your preferred format, attack style, deck colors through trial and error.

There are many ways to build decks that suit your unique style in the game, something you can only learn by playing the cards themselves.

## Choosing Decks

The aim and purpose of this book was to assist anyone in being able to pick up a deck and know how to interpret and build the deck you desire. Hopefully, you have a clearer understanding of what types, styles and colors are in a deck and how to use those against opponents in the game.

## Finding Cards

Additionally, the material about where to get cards themselves, build your deck and card strength through finding resources to assist with this process. Hopefully, this book has inspired you to find your own group or one on one opponent to try out and hone your "Magic The Gathering" skills.

# Thank You

As we reach the end of this book, I want to say thanks for reading this book.

I want to get this information out to as many people as possible. If you found this book helpful, I would greatly appreciate you leaving me a review on Amazon here. This helps others find the book as well.

I love hearing from readers so please get in touch via E-mail: cabpublishing1@gmail.com[5]

---

[5]mailto:cabpublishing1@gmail.com

# Disclaimer

This document is geared towards providing exact and reliable information in regards to the topic and issue covered. The publication is sold with the idea that the publisher is not required to render accounting, officially permitted, or otherwise, qualified services. If advice is necessary, legal or professional, a practiced individual in the profession should be ordered.

This information is not presented by a medical practicioner and is for educational and informational purposes only. The content is not intended as a substitute for professional medical advice, diagnosis, or treatment. Always seek the advice of your physician or other qualified health care provider with any questions you may have regarding a medical condition. Never disregard professional medical advice or delay in seeking it because of something you have read.

The information provided herein is stated to be truthful and consistent, in that any liability, in terms of inattention or otherwise, by any usage or abuse of any policies, processes, or directions contained within is the solitary and utter responsibility of the recipient reader. Under no circumstances will any legal responsibility or blame be held against the publisher for any reparation, damages, or monetary loss

# DISCLAIMER

due to the information herein, either directly or indirectly.

Last Updated: 1.Feb.2017

61133049R00019

Made in the USA
Lexington, KY
01 March 2017